THE WOUNDED KNEE
MASSACRE

NATIVE AMERICAN WAR

US History Non Fiction 4th Grade

Children's American History

BABY PROFESSOR
EDUCATION KIDS

Speedy Publishing LLC

40 E. Main St. #1156

Newark, DE 19711

www.speedypublishing.com

Copyright 2017

The last great fight of the war between Native Americans and white settlers in North America was in 1890 at Wounded Knee. Why did it happen, and what happened after? Read on and find out!

Native Americans Speaking To Settlers

NATIVE AMERICANS UNDER PRESSURE

European settlers in the "new world" had an uneasy relationship with the Native Americans who had lived there for tens of thousands of years. Sometimes the two peoples got on well, but at other times there was killing, theft, and other horrible deeds.

Native Americans saw the land, the forests, and the animals as a living community that they were part of, not something they owned.

*S*ettlers from Europe saw the land as something to be owned, developed, exploited, and eventually turned into money. These two attitudes were in direct conflict.

For sixty years after the first European settlement in Massachusetts, in 1620, the newcomers and the Native Americans struggled to find a balance. The tribes resented losing their land; some of the colonists thought the Native Americans were not even human, and should be wiped out. Read about the first big conflict at the end of this time of peace in the Baby Professor book King Philip's War.

Native American Tribe

The white settlers kept pushing west. They would make treaties with tribes, promising them "peace forever" and secure territory if the tribes would just give up another chunk of land. And then the settlers would break that treaty. The Native American tribes were weakened by diseases the Europeans brought, and did not have the weapons or fighting organization of the newcomers. So they fought as hard as they could, but they kept losing and having to retreat west.

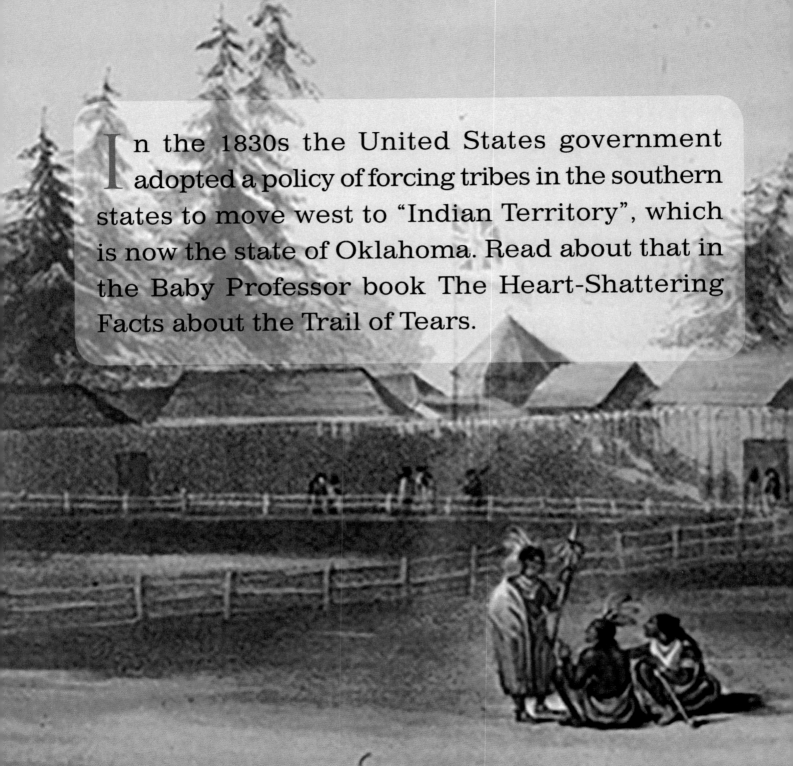

In the 1830s the United States government adopted a policy of forcing tribes in the southern states to move west to "Indian Territory", which is now the state of Oklahoma. Read about that in the Baby Professor book The Heart-Shattering Facts about the Trail of Tears.

After the Civil War (1861-65), the push west grew quickly. Hunters with rifles destroyed the buffalo herds many tribes relied on, and all tribes saw their territories continually shrinking.

White settlers gave cheap alcohol to the native people in exchange for beaver and buffalo skins, creating a generation of alcoholics who could no longer live in their traditional way.

LITTLE BIGHORN

A group of tribes made a great effort to push back the settlers, and to block the new railroad that was being built all the way across the country. The federal government sent the army to force the Native Americans onto reservations away from the land the white people wanted.

The Custer Fight

The last great battle of that effort was at the Little Bighorn River in June, 1876, when native fighters wiped out a detachment of the Seventh Cavalry under Civil War hero George Armstrong Custer. Read about that in the Baby Professor book What Happened Before, During, and After the Battle of the Little Bighorn?

THE GHOST DANCE

By the 1880s, the Native American tribes were in a desperate situation. Their numbers had shrunk, their land had shrunk, and there seemed to be no future for them.

Arapahoes performing the
Ghost Dance

In January, 1889, a Paiute shaman (holy man), Wovoka, had a vision. (Learn more about Native American spirituality in the Baby Professor book The World is Full of Spirits.) Wovoka said that God

appeared to him and described a beautiful future if the tribes united and resisted the spread of the new civilization.

Wovoka described and started a Ghost Dance ceremony. The ceremony would join the spirits of dead warriors with the spirits of the living Native Americans, to strengthen them to fight the white people. Wovoka said that the tribes would have to fight, with the help of the spirits of the dead, to win through to the peaceful future, full of buffalo, that he had seen in his vision.

Medicine man performing
a ghost dance

Sitting Bull

The teaching of the Ghost Dance spread quickly through many tribes. Chief Sitting Bull, who had been the leader of the forces that fought at the Little Bighorn, supported the Ghost Dance movement and brought many native people into it. The movement grew so that the majority of some tribes were committed Wovoka's vision.

White settlers became afraid that the tribes would rise up and kill all non-natives in the west. Federal government agents sent telegraph messages pleading for more soldiers and more action. In November, 1890, General Miles led 5,000 U.S. troops into the Dakotas to arrest leaders of the Ghost Dance movement.

Big Foot's band of Miniconjou Sioux

The beginning of the fight
at Wounded Knee

THE FIGHT AT WOUNDED KNEE

The army was afraid that Sitting Bull would lead the Lakota Sioux warriors out of their reservation to some hidden location where they could prepare to make war. The federal forces decided to arrest Sitting Bull. On December 15, 1890, as officers struggled with tribal warriors to get to the chief to arrest him, Sitting Bull was shot and killed.

B ig Foot, another chief, led a group of about 350 Lakota to join the encampment of Chief Red Cloud near Wounded Knee Creek. The U.S. cavalry caught up with the group and surrounded the camp.

Bigfoot Indian Chief

Wounded Knee Massacre Survivors

The troops arrested Red Cloud, who was too sick with pneumonia to fight back. On December 29, the army placed Hotchkiss guns, rapid-fire weapons like machine guns, on a hill near the camp to threaten the native people, and federal cavalry units surrounded the camp.

A medicine man began the Ghost Dance ritual, calling on the spirits to scatter the cavalry troops like the handfuls of dust he threw in the air.

He told the native fighters that the soldiers' bullets would not touch them, but would fly over them and disappear into the prairie.

Accounts differ about what happened next. The troops started to move into the camp, going from tent to tent in search of weapons. They took not only weapons, but knives and axes, tools the native people would need to survive.

Some reports say that a deaf Native American had a weapon under his blanket and the soldiers tried to take it away. The deaf man may not have understood what was happening. In any case, he resisted. There was a struggle, and someone fired the first shot.

Medicine Man

The U.S. soldiers started firing into the camp from all sides, with the machine guns firing into the teepees even though the gunners could not tell if there were fighters or children inside. The Lakota were surrounded and had almost no weapons, so they could hardly fight back.

Chief Big Foot died where he was lying on the ground. Children who had been playing together now lay dead together. After

Lakota Sioux

a few minutes, between 150 and 300 Lakota Sioux were dead, half of them women and children. Twenty-five U.S. soldiers also died.

AFTERMATH

A few Lakota managed to escape the slaughter and hide in the hills. The federal government held an inquiry, and ruled that the soldiers had acted correctly. In fact, the government awarded twenty Medals of Honor, the highest military award, to participants in the massacre.

This was not the last battle between the federal forces and warriors of the Native American tribes, but it is considered as the battle that marked the end of the Indian Wars and the end of Native American independence.

After Wounded Knee, most Native Americans were either restricted to reservations, or forcibly assimilated into white culture, giving up their traditions, including the Ghost Dance. To learn more about reservation life, read the Baby Professor book Are Indian Reservations part of the US?

Before the Europeans arrived in North America, the Native American civilizations had as many as 18 million members. By 1900, the number of Native Americans had fallen below 250,000 people.

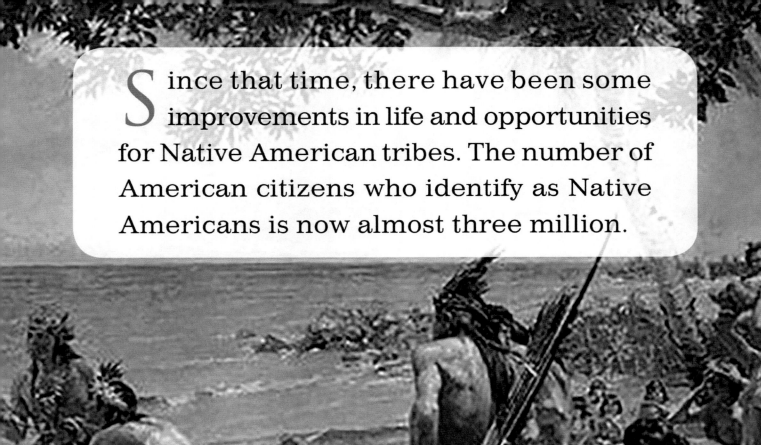

Since that time, there have been some improvements in life and opportunities for Native American tribes. The number of American citizens who identify as Native Americans is now almost three million.

The arrival of Christopher Colombus to America

Wounded Knee

ANOTHER WOUNDED KNEE

In February, 1973, members of the American Indian Movement occupied the town of Wounded Knee on the Pine Ridge Indian Reservation, near the site of the massacre, to protest the treatment of Native Americans by the federal government. They were also upset by what they felt were corrupt actions by the leaders of the reservation.

The occupation lasted over seventy days, and involved confrontations and exchanges of gunfire with United States Marshals. Two Native Americans were shot and killed, and one U.S. Marshal was paralyzed.

Wounded Knee encampment

The standoff drew attention to the failures of the federal government to live up to its promises, made in solemn treaties, to the Native

American tribes. The leaders of the occupation were tried on charges of conspiracy, but were found not guilty.

THE FIRST PEOPLES ARE NOT GONE

Native American tribes do not live as they did before European settlement began in North America, and many tribes and cultures have disappeared. However, Native Americans have played, and still play, an important role in United States history. Read Baby Professor books like Getting to Know the Great Native American Tribes and The 8 Most Famous Native Americans to learn more about the first residents of North America.

Visit

BABY PROFESSOR
EDUCATION KIDS

www.BabyProfessorBooks.com

to download Free Baby Professor eBooks and view
our catalog of new and exciting Children's Books

Made in the USA
Las Vegas, NV
18 May 2024

90078613R00040